A LETTER FOR LENT

*A group Lent course
based on Paul's letter
to the Colossians*

A LETTER FOR LENT

PATRICK COGHLAN

**kevin
mayhew**

kevin
mayhew

First published in Great Britain in 2017 by Kevin Mayhew Ltd
Buxhall, Stowmarket, Suffolk IP14 3BW
Tel: +44 (0) 1449 737978 Fax: +44 (0) 1449 737834
E-mail: info@kevinmayhew.com

www.kevinmayhew.com

9 8 7 6 5 4 3 2 1 0

ISBN 978 1 84867 934 4
Catalogue No. 1501573

Cover design by Rob Mortonson
© Image used under licence from Shutterstock Inc.
Edited by Helen Jones
Typeset by Angela Selfe

Printed and bound in Great Britain

Contents

Personal Bible Study for
Monday to Friday of Holy Week

Onesimus' story (Colossians 4:7-18; Philemon 1-25)

About the author

Patrick is the minister at Worstead Baptist Church in Meeting Hill (North Norfolk). He is also a trustee and the chaplain of Aylsham and district Care Trust (ACT), and the manager of ACT Counselling Services – both of which are based at the ACT Centre, in Aylsham. ACT is a Christian community care charity, and does a lot of work with older people. The ACT Centre is part of the St Michael's Care Complex.

In his work as a minister, chaplain and counsellor, Patrick has had considerable experience of working with people of most age groups, in the context of providing ministry and care.

Patrick is married to June and they have two grown-up children – Rachel and Jonathan. For his leisure, Patrick enjoys quality family time, walking the dog, horse riding and riding his red motorcycle.

Patrick has been an enthusiastic author for many years, having had his first book published in 2001. He has written a variety of Christian resources for different age groups, and some family novels.

Introduction

A Letter for Lent is a six-session group Bible study course for use during Lent, which looks at Paul's letter to the Colossians. In addition, there is a meditative personal Bible study course based on Paul's letter to Philemon, to be used on Monday to Friday of Holy Week.

Lent is both a time to prepare for the coming of Easter, and our response to it; and also a time for reviewing our own daily Christian walk and the spiritual lives of our *fellowships/congregations*.

The group Bible study course is an easy-to-follow, off-the-page resource, encouraging all the members of the group to participate in the discussion (including the sharing of personal testimony and life experience) and also in the prayer time. The application is both for the members of the group as individuals, but also collectively for the *fellowships/congregations* represented.

The personal Bible study course, which is based on Paul's letter to Philemon (looking at the story about Onesimus), focuses mainly on our personal spiritual journeys. It is more meditative and encourages a time to be still and quiet in God's presence each day. On Good Friday the focus is on making a prayer response to the Bible study's content and what God is saying to the reader through it.

It might be helpful for all the members of the group to have a pen and notebook to hand, for use as a personal journal during the course. Points of interest, words from God, matters for prayer and written prayers to be read out in the prayer times can be jotted down in it.

Format

The group Bible study course for Lent is based around the concept of letter writing, and is in six sessions:

Welcome: includes the suggestion of a way to thoughtfully prepare for the study.

A letter in the post: introduces the theme of the session. It begins with a fictional letter to be read out loud; and continues with a series of linked discussion points for the group to consider.

Opening prayer: is a prayer to be read out loud by one of the members of the group. There is a link between this prayer and the theme of the session, as well as to the overall study.

A letter from Paul: refers to Paul's letter to the Colossians; and gives the Bible references for the passage to be read out loud by one of the members of the group, and on which the session is based.

A letter to the Church: is the material to be used for the Bible study section of the session. It is a series of discussion points that are based around how Paul's teaching applies to the Christian Church today. There are some additional relevant Bible references included.

A letter to you: is intended specifically to be a challenge for each member of the group individually. The group leader will allow a few minutes of silence for everyone to consider this challenge and maybe write their thoughts down in their journals. An opportunity will follow for people to share anything they feel is appropriate.

A letter to God: is a prayer response. During the course of the six sessions a variety of different ways of praying are explored, although some groups might just choose to have a completely open prayer time – out loud or silently.

Refreshments and prayer ministry: The group may or may not choose to have a time of refreshments. It allows time for fellowship and an opportunity for further discussion and prayer, but some members of the group may need to get home for other commitments. It is always good to advertise a set finishing time for the study part of the session for that reason. Under this heading a suggestion is made for an optional topic of conversation.

The meditative personal Bible study course is based around the retelling of the story about Onesimus and is in five sessions:

- **Bible reading:** A Bible reference is given for a passage to be read, to lead into the session.

- **Onesimus' story:** is the ongoing story about Onesimus in bite-size chunks. It has been expanded and a degree of imagination has been carefully added, as we do not have a huge amount of information about Onesimus in the Bible.

- **Your story:** is the Bible study part of the session, focused on the story about Onesimus and its application.

- **Key thoughts about...:** are a few carefully chosen phrases from the session, which act to reinforce its content. They are picked up again in the session for Good Friday, as the basis for the prayer response.

- **Resting in prayer:** is a time to be still and quiet in God's presence. It encourages an attitude of thanksgiving but avoiding saying too many words.

GROUP LENT COURSE

A letter of encouragement
(Colossians 1:1-14)

Welcome:

As a time of preparation for the session ahead, ask someone in the group to read Psalm 150 out loud – a wonderful Psalm of encouragement! Then, during the playing of some Christian instrumental music, spend some time considering and silently giving thanks to the great Creator God, that he is also a personal God, wanting a relationship with each one of us.

A letter in the post! (Introduction to session):

Dear neighbour,

Just a quick note to say a big 'thank you' for helping me out the other day. It was really appreciated. I am not that great at asking for help, or even admitting that I need it. I am so grateful to you for your act of kindness; it made a big difference.

Thanks again!

- What does it feel like to receive an informal letter from a neighbour, friend or family member? It could be a letter of thanks, a letter requesting help or an informative letter passing on greetings and news. Share your experiences with the other members of the group.

- Does a letter received through the post or delivered by hand feel any different from receiving a text or email? If so, why?

- How would you feel if you received the above letter?

Opening prayer:

Our loving, heavenly Father,
Thank you for family, friends and neighbours.
Thank you for the joy of receiving a letter, text or email of greeting, encouragement or news.
Thank you for leading Paul to write those letters that we are familiar with in the New Testament – of such value to all generations, including us today.
Be with us now; fill us afresh with your Holy Spirit; and guide our thoughts and responses as we begin to look at Paul's letter to the Colossians.
In Jesus' name,
Amen.

A letter from Paul (Paul's letter to the Colossians):
Read Colossians 1:1-14.

A letter to the Church (How Paul's teaching applies to the Christian Church today):

Giving thanks for each other (Colossians 1:3-8):

- Each one of you probably thanks God for your family and friends on a regular basis; but do you thank God for your fellow Christians and how he is at work in their lives – both in your particular *fellowship/congregation*, but also for those belonging to the wider Christian Church?

- What kind of things would you thank God for, in each other?

- We are all created in God's image (Genesis 1:26), but at the same time completely unique. Discuss.

- Paul refers to several ways of encouraging each other to live out the Christian life of love and witness. Talk about these together.

Pleasing God (Colossians 1:9-14):

- What can we do to please God?

- 'Because of my Christian faith, I don't always feel that I fit in *at work/in my neighbourhood/socially/ etc.*' Discuss, sharing something of your personal experiences (if you feel able to).

- Talk about your feelings concerning the conflict that could arise between conforming to society, making compromises, trying to be accepted in work and social situations – and living God's way.

- How should we be praying for each other?

- In Colossians 1:4-6, Paul speaks about having heard good things concerning the Colossian Church. If Paul were around today, what might he hear concerning the *fellowships/congregations* you represent?

A letter to you (A question that is directed specifically to you individually):

- Giving thanks for each other, and for what God is doing in our lives, is all about loving, valuing and accepting;

and being loved, valued and accepted. How does that feel from your perspective?

(Afterwards, allow a few minutes for members of the group to share anything that particularly came out of this time of personal meditation for them – if they would like to.)

A letter to God (Either write your own prayer responding to what God has said to you in this session, and then pray it, or else use the following prayer headings to lead a time of spontaneous open prayer – aloud or silently):

Our loving, heavenly Father,
Thank you for each other and the ways in which you are working in our lives . . .
Thank you for the ways in which we are able to receive encouragement; and for the ways in which we are able to give encouragement . . .
Thank you for the wonderfully uplifting letters that Paul wrote and for all we can learn from them today...
Help us to say and do only those things that are pleasing to you . . .
Help us to be prepared to be different for the sake of the kingdom . . .
Equip us for times of persecution and conflict for the sake of the kingdom . . .
We pray that the news other people hear about our *fellowships/congregations* will be good and honouring to you . . .
In Jesus' name,
Amen.

Refreshments and prayer ministry:

As you enjoy the time of refreshments together, you might like to encourage each other by praying informally for each other, in pairs or small groups. Ask each other what they would like you to pray about, beforehand.

Getting to know God
(Colossians 1:15-23)

Welcome:

As a time of preparation for the session ahead, ask someone in the group to read Job 42:1-6 out loud – take note of verse 5! Then, during the playing of some Christian instrumental music, spend some time considering the significance of Job's words. He is effectively saying that through his suffering he has moved on from just knowing about God, to knowing God personally.

A letter in the post! (Introduction to session):

Hello my dear pen friend,

How long is it now since we began writing to each other? Longer than I care to remember! And yet we have never met face to face – but I must admit, I still feel that I know you. You have told me so much about yourself in your letters – and some of the photographs you have sent to me have really made me smile. But I wanted to say what a joy it was to meet your son last week, while he was on holiday in this area – shame about the weather! I feel that I know you even better now, through meeting with him and experiencing the family likeness. I look forward to hearing from you soon.

Keep writing!

- Talk about the different ways in which we get to know another person better, e.g. writing letters to each other is just one way.

- What do you think makes a good friendship?

- How often we hear phrases like, 'Isn't he like his father?' Discuss family likenesses.

Opening prayer:

Loving God,
Thank you for the opportunities to enter into friendships.
Thank you that there are many different ways to get to
know other people better.
Thank you that Paul's intention is that we get to know you
better; and that his letter to the Colossian Church helps us
to understand how to do that.
Be with us now; fill us afresh with the Holy Spirit; and
guide our thoughts and responses as we continue to look at
Paul's letter to the Colossians.
In Jesus' name,
Amen.

A letter from Paul (Paul's letter to the Colossians):
Read Colossians 1:15-23.

A letter to the Church (How Paul's teaching applies to the Christian Church today):

Jesus is just like his Father (Colossians 1:15-20):

- Read the following passages of Scripture, linking them in with the humanity of Jesus, e.g. the humility of his birth (Luke 2:1-7), the life of a servant

(Matthew 8:18-22), and the suffering around his death (Isaiah 53:4-6).

- In contrast to the humanity of Jesus, in Colossians 1:15-20 Paul is focusing on the divinity of Jesus: his active presence in creation and its sustenance, his sovereignty, his position as head of the Church, the *fullness of God* dwelling within him and that he is the way to salvation (see also John 1:1-2). Discuss.

- Talk about the family likeness of God.

- How can we get to know God better through Jesus, with reference to that family likeness (see Colossians 1:15 and John 14:8-9)?

A firm foundation for life (Colossians 1:21-23):

- Jesus talks about building a house on the rock (Matthew 7:24-29); and Peter speaks about the Cornerstone (1 Peter 2:1-10) – both references to building our lives on the firm foundation of following Jesus. In John 14:6 Jesus confirms that he is the only way to the Father and the only way for us to receive eternal life. What are your comments on these different analogies and their significance?

- In Colossians 1:21-23 Paul speaks about 'the hope promised by the gospel'. There is a lot in these three verses; what particularly stands out for you?

- In what ways do your *fellowships/congregations* encourage people to get to know God better? Think in terms of ministry and outreach.

A letter to you (A question that is directed specifically to you individually):

- As we learn more about Jesus through Scripture and our personal journey with him, we get to know God the Father better and experience the Holy Spirit working in our lives to an even greater extent. Consider carefully your relationship with Jesus, God the Father and the Holy Spirit.

(Afterwards, allow a few minutes for members of the group to share anything that particularly came out of this time of personal meditation for them – if they would like to.)

A letter to God (Either write your own prayer responding to what God has said to you in this session, and then pray it, or else use the following prayer headings to lead a time of spontaneous open prayer – aloud or silently):

Father God,
Thank you that it is your desire for us to get to know
you better ...
Thank you that we can learn more about you as we study
the life and teaching of Jesus from the Bible, and as we walk
closer to him day by day ...
Thank you that Jesus is the firm foundation, on which we
can all base our lives ...
Help us to get to know you better as we get to know Jesus
better, and through the power of the indwelling Holy Spirit ...
Help us during those challenging times in our lives *(silently
name those situations)* ...

We pray for the ministry and outreach of our *fellowships/ congregations*, that they will be effective in helping us – and those in our neighbourhood – to get to know you and Jesus more, and to be filled with the Holy Spirit . . .
In Jesus' name,
Amen.

Refreshments and prayer ministry

As you enjoy the time of refreshments together, you might like to share some personal testimony, focusing on how and when you have got to know God better. It is possible that some of you have had a similar experience of realisation to that of Job.

The Church
(Colossians 1:24–2:5)

Welcome:

As a time of preparation for the session ahead, ask someone in the group to read Acts 2:42-47 out loud. Then, during the playing of some Christian instrumental music, meditate upon life in the early Christian Church, as described in the passage, and how that applies to the Church today.

A letter in the post! (Introduction to session):

To my lifelong buddy,

Guess what I spent my weekend doing – up to my knees in dust and cobwebs? I had decided to clear out the attic, having already put it off for about three years. And while I was doing it, I discovered an old chocolate box full of photographs and newspaper cuttings. As I was sifting through them, I was reminded of you; and the times we spent together during our childhood. We had so much fun and laughter; but there were also some sad and traumatic times as well. But our friendship survived it all.

Keep smiling.

- Share some thoughts about a particular article, letter or photograph that brings back fond memories to you, and why.

- If you feel able, speak to the rest of the group about a friend who stuck by you during a difficult time in your life. What gave that relationship the strength to survive?

- Discuss the kind of qualities and resources that we generally associate with endurance during the good and the bad times in life.

Opening prayer:

Father God,
Thank you for those friends who have supported us
during difficult and traumatic times in our lives – for their
compassion, love and care.
Thank you that Paul's intention is that we should learn to
depend on you during the good and the bad experiences
in our lives; and the letter to the Colossians helps us to
understand how to do that better.
Be with us now; fill us afresh with the Holy Spirit; and
guide our thoughts and responses as we continue to look at
Paul's letter to the Colossians.
In Jesus' name,
Amen.

A letter from Paul (Paul's letter to the Colossians):
Read Colossians 1:24–2:5.

A letter to the Church (How Paul's teaching applies to the Christian Church today):

In good times and bad (Colossians 1:24):

- In Colossians 1:24, Paul refers to the inevitability of suffering when we serve Jesus in love and witness, as part of the Church. The Christian life is not an easy one; as such, it is not without suffering and persecution. Let's not fool ourselves that we can be followers of Jesus in complete freedom in the UK: that we can live according to the teaching of the Bible; that we can overtly proclaim our faith; or that we can challenge issues of the day without fear of persecution. Discuss.

• Paul also speaks about rejoicing in suffering in that very same verse. That whole concept is probably quite alien to modern society. What does this say about living in relationship with the Triune God and depending on him? Share your own personal experiences if you feel able to.

Belonging (Colossians 1:24–2:5):

• In Colossians 1:24, Paul speaks about 'Christ's . . . body, that is, the church' – one body, many parts, all equal in importance (see 1 Corinthians 12:12-31). What is your understanding of the concept of the Body of Christ, with a particular reference to belonging?

• Talk about what it means for us all to be unique and how the Church benefits from that, in the context of also being created in the image of God (Genesis 1:26).

• In Colossians 2:1-5, Paul speaks about being 'united in love', the 'hidden . . . treasures of wisdom and knowledge' and the 'firmness of . . . faith'. Discuss with particular reference to the words unity, hidden and firmness.

- What gives you a real feeling of belonging to your *fellowships/congregations?* Is there anything that would make you feel that sense of belonging even more strongly?

A letter to you (A question that is directed specifically to you individually):

- Belonging to a *fellowship/congregation* – and indeed belonging to the wider Christian Church – is not just about what it offers you; it is also about what you are prepared to offer. Think about being willing to give things like time, commitment, perseverance, endurance and service.

(Afterwards, allow a few minutes for members of the group to share anything that particularly came out of this time of personal meditation for them – if they would like to.)

A letter to God (Either write your own prayer responding to what God has said to you in this session, and then pray it, or else use the following prayers, linked with the leads in):

- Silently to God, name any areas of suffering, persecution or difficulty in your lives at the present time.

Almighty God,
Thank you that you are in control of that which you have created and you are working out your eternal plan of hope.
You have heard what the areas are in our lives that we are particularly struggling with at the moment, in terms of suffering, persecution and difficulty.
Grant us your strength and wisdom, through the power of your Holy Spirit, to enable us not only to endure those

struggles, but also to come out rejoicing and glorifying you.
In Jesus' name,
Amen.

- Silently meditate on the whole concept of what it means
  to belong to an individual *fellowship/congregation*; but at
  the same time to be part of the wider Christian Church
  – the Body of Christ, the family of God and God's eternal
  kingdom – through our personal relationship with Jesus.

Loving Lord Jesus,
Thank you that you love us so much that you gave your life
on the cross, paying the penalty for our sin.
Thank you that you rose again from the dead, and you are
alive today.
Thank you that through a personal relationship with you,
based on repentance and with faith, we enter into your
eternal kingdom and we become part of the family of God –
and belong to your Church.
Help and equip us to take on the responsibility of being
part of your Body – called to serve you in the world today –
including in our individual *fellowships/congregations*.
In your name we pray.
Amen.

- Silently to God, name some of the resources, including
  spiritual gifts, talents and abilities, which you are using
  already, or offering to use, to help build the kingdom
  in your local *fellowships/congregations* and as part of the
  wider Christian Church.

Our loving, heavenly Father,
Thank you that you have created each of us to be unique
and with a wonderful variety of resources that we can use
in your service to help build the kingdom. Anoint those
resources, and grant us a willingness to offer them up to
you to be used to further your purposes in the *fellowships/
congregations* that we belong to and as part of the wider
Christian Church.
We pray for your blessing upon the *fellowships/congregations*
represented here today and the ministry of those
fellowships/congregations.
Help us in our daily lives of love and witness to further your
kingdom and glorify your name, pointing others towards Jesus.
In his name,
Amen.

- Silently to God, name people known to you who are
  suffering in some way, and situations involving suffering
  locally, nationally and beyond.

Lord, we place these people, who are suffering in some way,
into your hands, and ask that you will surround them with
your love and care.
Also, be in those situations we have named involving
suffering locally, nationally and worldwide.
In Jesus' name,
Amen.

Refreshments and prayer ministry
As you enjoy the time of refreshments together, you might like
to chat about how you like to praise and worship God. What is
your preferred style? Remember that diversity in the style and
content of praise and worship is not the same as division!

Continuing in the faith
(Colossians 2:6-23)

Welcome:
As a time of preparation for the session ahead, listen to, and consider, the words of a worship song (your choice) all about faith.

A letter in the post! (Introduction to session):

Dear athletic friend,

I am writing this to you as your trainer. There is not long to go now before you run the marathon. I know you have trained hard and consistently, and admittedly suffered a few blisters and minor injuries, but I sensed last time we met for training that you were considering cancelling your entry. Mate! Don't give up now; you're nearly there.

Keep running!

- You might have received a similar letter yourself at some time in your life: a letter urging you to stick with something. If you feel able to, share your experience of feeling like giving up on something you have undertaken. It might be a course of further education, a particular career, a task in the house or garden, a hobby, etc. What was the outcome?

- Talk in general terms about the kind of things that can cause us to feel like giving up with a particular task or interest.

- What might help us to keep going at such a time?

Opening prayer:

Faithful God,
Thank you for those people whom you have set around us
to help us to persevere when we are tempted to give up.
Thank you that in Paul's letter to the Colossians he urges us
to continue to live out the Christian life of love and witness,
and to build up our relationship with Jesus.
Be with us now; fill us afresh with your Holy Spirit; and
guide our thoughts and responses as we continue to look at
Paul's letter to the Colossians.
In Jesus' name,
Amen.

A letter from Paul (Paul's letter to the Colossians):
Read Colossians 2:6-23.

A letter to the Church (How Paul's teaching applies to the
Christian Church today):

Keeping up the momentum (Colossians 2:6-23):

- I am sure that we have all started new hobbies, new
  training courses or new jobs; and really enjoyed
  them initially, full of enthusiasm. We acquired all
  the equipment for the new hobby, bought all the
  books and stationery for the new course, or were
  fitted with the uniform for the new job. But then
  a few weeks down the line realised: it's not really
  the hobby for me; it's not really the course of study
  for me; or it's not really the job for me. Starting
  something new can be very exciting and exhilarating
  but it is so easy to lose enthusiasm and momentum

after a time. Paul warns us not to do that same thing in the context of our Christian faith (Colossians 2:6-7). Discuss.

• It could be that you have been a Christian for a long time: there have been disappointments, struggles and opposition; maybe there have been times when you have become disillusioned, or even complacent or apathetic. What was it that kept you going in your faith at the time?

• Our daily walk with Jesus is vital to our spiritual well-being and effectiveness in service. This is highlighted in Colossians 2:19 where Paul once again takes up the analogy of the Body of Christ. Examine the analogy in the context in which it is used here.

Relating with Jesus (Colossians 2:6-23):

• In Colossians 2:7 Paul encourages us to be 'rooted' in Jesus, to be 'built up' in Jesus, to be 'established in the faith', and to be 'abounding in thanksgiving'. What ideas do these phrases conjure up in your minds?

• Talk about the importance of basing our beliefs and lifestyles on the Bible – particularly on the life and teaching of Jesus – expressed in Colossians 2:8.

• Bearing in mind Paul's words in Colossians 2:8, would you describe the teaching in your *fellowships/congregations* to be based firmly on Scripture?

A letter to you (A question that is directed specifically to you individually):

- Are you 'abounding in thanksgiving' (Colossians 2:7), or is that something you struggle with at times? Paul encourages us to be thankful to God, because he believes it is important to our spiritual health and well-being. Maybe it is something that most of us need to work on.

(Afterwards, allow a few minutes for members of the group to share anything that particularly came out of this time of personal meditation for them – if they would like to.)

A letter to God (Either write your own prayer responding to what God has said to you in this session, and then pray it, or else use the following prayers, linked with the leads in):

- Silently meditate on what it means to be 'rooted' in Jesus:

Our Lord and Saviour Jesus Christ,
Thank you for dying on the cross, paying the penalty for our sin – and that you rose again.
Thank you that we can all have a personal relationship with you.
Help us to walk close to you, day by day: to effectively have deep roots in you – enabling us to stand firm during opposition, persecution, temptation, and difficult or discouraging times in our lives, and so that we might be spiritually nourished.
In Jesus' name,
Amen.

- Silently to God, name people who are currently facing opposition, persecution or temptation, or who are going through difficult or discouraging times in their lives (include yourself if it is appropriate):

Father God,
Thank you that through the power of the indwelling Holy Spirit you guide and strengthen us as we face opposition, persecution, temptation, difficulties and discouragements in our lives.
We place into your hands those who we have named, including ourselves and ask that you will guide and strengthen us as we deal with one or other of those issues at the present time.
In Jesus' name,
Amen.

- Silently meditate on what it means to be 'built up' in Jesus:

Lord Jesus,
Thank you that we can be built up spiritually, through following you. We are restored in our relationship with the Father; cleansed, transformed, strengthened and empowered by the Holy Spirit; and clothed in your righteousness. You have called us, you teach us, you guide us, and you have set us a perfect example to follow.
Help us to be focused on you; make us a loving, prayerful, scripturally based, serving people.
Heal and build us up from the sickness of sin.
In your name,
Amen.

- Silently meditate on what it means to be 'established in the faith':

Heavenly Father,
Thank you that all growth is from you.
Help us in our life's journeys to become increasingly
spiritually mature and strengthened in our faith.
In Jesus' name,
Amen.

- Silently to God, name any areas of your life in which you struggle to be 'abounding in thanksgiving':

Almighty God,
We thank you for *(as a group name out loud things for which you are thankful to God).*
Help us to be thankful in all things.
In Jesus' name,
Amen.

Refreshments and prayer ministry

As you enjoy the time of refreshments together, you might like to chat about any projects you are currently working on for the Lord – it could well be a joint project with others in your *fellowship/congregation.*

On earth as it is in heaven
(Colossians 3:1–4:1)

Welcome:

As a time of preparation for the session ahead, ask someone in the group to read Matthew 6:5-15 out loud. Then, during the playing of some Christian instrumental music, meditate upon the significance of verse 10.

A letter in the post! (Introduction to session):

Greetings!

It was great to see you last week, when we bumped into each other in town. How long had it been since we previously met? Too long! And you were right, we have known each other for over fifty years. It only seems like yesterday that we first met at school. It was quite a surprise to see how like your father you have become now. I remember him well, from when I used to come round to your house during our school holidays: his looks, his mannerisms, those little phrases he used to come out with and his strict value system. It's all there in you now. You're almost like his double. But it was really good to have a chat. We mustn't leave it so long before we catch up again.

Keep in touch!

- How much do you take after your parents and in what ways?

- How much of the family likeness in us do you think is hereditary? And how much do you think is learned? Which aspects would you attribute to which? Discuss.

- Talk about any aspects of the family likeness that you have deliberately strived to achieve in your life. What are they? And why were they important to you? You might discover some similarities amongst the group.

Opening prayer:

Our loving, heavenly Father,
Thank you for our earthly families.
Thank you for the opportunity to be part of your family.
Thank you that Paul's letter to the Colossians has a lot to
say about taking on your likeness and the joy of being part
of your family – and getting on with each other.
Be with us now; fill us afresh with your Holy Spirit; and
guide our thoughts and responses as we continue to look at
Paul's letter to the Colossians.
In Jesus' name,
Amen.

A letter from Paul (Paul's letter to the Colossians):
Read Colossians 3:1–4:1.

A letter to the Church (How Paul's teaching applies to the Christian Church today):

Focusing on God and taking on the family likeness
(Colossians 3:1-17):

- Christianity is about relationship and lifestyle. Discuss.

- In Colossian 3:1-2 Paul instructs 'seek the things that are above' and 'set your minds on things that are above'. Paul seems to be deliberately differentiating between our hearts and our minds. The things of our hearts refer to feelings, emotions, sources of motivation, desire, etc. Whereas the things of our minds refers to thoughts, learning, choices we make, etc. How can we focus our hearts and minds 'on things that are above'?

- Though we were created in the image of God (Genesis 1:26) our life's journey is still about learning from the teaching of Scripture and the example of Jesus – striving to progressively become more Christlike (the family likeness of God). Talk about the role that prayer, Bible study, teaching and the indwelling Holy Spirit have in this process.

- In Colossians 3:9-14, Paul is effectively saying, 'Becoming a Christian is like changing from one set of clothes to another. Take the dirty clothes off, and put the clean ones on.' He says, 'Clothe yourselves with compassion, kindness, humility, meekness and patience' (verse 12b); and 'above all, clothe yourselves with love' (verse 14a). Of course, we are very distinctive by the clothes that we wear, including in a spiritual context: people notice them. What do you think?

Getting on with each other (Colossians 3:18–4:1):

- Primarily Colossians 3:18–4:1 is about relationships; it is very similar to Ephesians 5:21–6:9. Paul is laying down some ground rules for us, as Christians, to encourage us to get on with each other. Give some hypothetical examples of ways in which people can fall out in the Church, highlighting possible causes, for example, lack of communication.

- Colossians 3:18–4:1 is all about love, care, encouragement, respect, safety, trust, getting on together . . . and striving to glorify God in our relationships. Talk about how this is illustrated in the way Paul speaks about the various relationships.

- 'Fall outs' or disagreements prevent a *fellowship/congregation* from experiencing the kind of growth and blessing that it could be experiencing. Discuss.

A letter to you (A question that is directed specifically to you individually):

- What do the 'spiritual' clothes that you wear say to others about you and your faith? And what do they say to others about Jesus?

(Afterwards, allow a few minutes for members of the group to share anything that particularly came out of this time of personal meditation for them – if they would like to.)

A letter to God (Pick a prayer that is appropriate for you, personalise it if you would like to, and then say it out loud):

Almighty, Creator God.
Thank you that you want a relationship with us all, and that you made it possible through Jesus.
Help us to walk more closely with you, day by day. *(Name any particular areas with which you struggle, for example,*

being more disciplined in prayer, Bible study, attending church, service, etc.)
In Jesus' name,
Amen.

Heavenly Father,
Thank you for the example that Jesus has set us in all things. Help us to follow that example and live the kind of lifestyle that is furthering of the kingdom and glorifying to your name. *(Name any areas of your lifestyle with which you struggle to live up to God's standards, or areas in which you feel we all need to be particularly vigilant.)*
In Jesus' name,
Amen.

Loving God,
Help us to focus our hearts and minds on the things that are of you. *(Name some of those things.)*
In Jesus' name,
Amen.

Almighty God,
Thank you that you created us all in your image.
Help us to allow the indwelling Holy Spirit to restore that image within us, even though it has been damaged by sin. Recreate us. *(Elaborate on the characteristics of God and how they apply to our lives: sovereignty, creativity, righteousness, and the ability to relate to others – to love and to be loved.)*
In Jesus' name,
Amen.

Lord Jesus.
Help us to be more like you. *(Name areas of Christlikeness, or God family likeness, that you particularly aspire to personally.)*
Amen.

Lord and Saviour Jesus Christ,
Help us to wear the kind of spiritual clothes that will get noticed for the right reasons. *(Elaborate on being clothed with compassion, kindness, humility, meekness, patience and love.)*
In Jesus' name,
Amen.

Lord Jesus,
All our relationships with other people are only as good as our relationship is with you.
Help us to walk closer to you, day by day: to allow the Holy Spirit to work freely in our lives and to be obedient to the Father.
Fill us with your love, gentleness and encouragement to share with others.
Give us the courage and graciousness to say 'sorry'.
Have your healing touch upon those relationships that have been broken. *(Invite members of the group to join with you in silently naming to God any relationships that need his healing touch.)*
In your name,
Amen

Loving, heavenly Father,
Fill us with your love; help us to be caring; grant us an encouraging spirit; help us to be respectful to others; and let us be worthy of the trust others place in us.

Let our church *fellowships/congregations* be safe environments. Help us to 'get on' with each other. *(Name any non-sensitive areas like communication that might need improving.)*
In Jesus' name,
Amen.

Lord Jesus,
Help us to be good witnesses to others in word and deed so that others may see you in the way that we live our lives. *(Name any areas of witness that you feel nervous about, for example, speaking about your faith, answering questions about the Bible, or not yielding to peer pressure.)*
In your name,
Amen.

Refreshments and prayer ministry
As you enjoy the time of refreshments together, you might like to chat about the value of the Lord's Prayer in years gone by, when it was a prayer which most people in the United Kingdom probably knew off by heart. Has that changed?

Aspirations
(Colossians 4:2-6)

Welcome:
As a time of preparation for the session ahead, listen to and consider the words of a worship song (your choice), all about the Christian journey.

A letter in the post! (Introduction to session):

Dear Sir,

This is just a brief letter to update you on my year out from university – travelling the world. I am in Canada at the moment, hoping to get some work for a few weeks. And then, when I have saved up some more money, I will be moving on again. Not quite sure where I shall be heading for next. It's quite an adventure – an ongoing and exciting journey full of surprises. But I will be 'enjoying' your lectures again in the autumn – for my final year! Looking forward to it – I think.

See you!

- Talk about a journey you have been on. Maybe you have had a gap year to travel the world; or perhaps you have been on a memorable summer holiday. What were your aspirations for the trip? Chat about each other's journeys.

- How would you describe your feelings at the beginning, middle and end of the journey?

- Some journeys are purely to get to our destination; others follow a carefully planned route, where the journey is almost as important as reaching the destination. Discuss.

Opening prayer:

Our loving, heavenly Father,
Thank you for those journeys we have made that bring back fond memories.
Thank you that as followers of Jesus we are on the
Christian journey of love and witness – heading towards the destination of your eternal, heavenly kingdom.
Thank you that in Paul's letter to the Colossians he speaks about things we should aspire to whilst on that journey.
Be with us now; fill us afresh with your Holy Spirit; and guide our thoughts and responses as we continue to look at Paul's letter to the Colossians.
In Jesus' name,
Amen.

A letter from Paul (Paul's letter to the Colossians):
Read Colossians 4:2-6.

A letter to the Church (How Paul's teaching applies to the Christian Church today):

Prayer (Colossians 4:2-4):

- There seems to be earnestness when Paul talks about prayer. In Romans 12:12b he commands: 'Persevere in prayer.' In Ephesians 6:18 he instructs: 'Pray in the Spirit at all times in every prayer and supplication.

To that end keep alert and always persevere in supplication for all the saints.' In Philippians 4:6b he says: 'But in everything by prayer and supplication . . . let your requests be made to God.' I am sure that we are all familiar with Paul's words in 1 Thessalonians 5:17: 'Pray without ceasing.' And in Colossians 4:2a he pleads: 'Devote yourselves to prayer.' Discuss the importance of prayer in our Christian journeys.

- Using what James says at the end of his letter (James 5:13-20) as a starting point, talk about prayer.

- How comfortable do you feel about prayer? How do you feel about praying on your own in a quiet place; praying on the go in the busyness of everyday life; praying with others in a quiet place; praying with others in the corner of a busy place; praying over the phone with others – and even text prayers; formal prayer; or informal prayer? Are you as organised as you would like to be in your prayer life? Share your thoughts.

Qualities to aspire towards (Colossians 4:5-6):

- In Colossians 4:5 Paul instructs: 'Conduct yourselves wisely towards outsiders, making the most of the time.' That might mean: doing the right thing; an act of kindness or generosity; a timely word of testimony; the acceptance of others; helping others to feel valued; or a word of encouragement. Discuss.

- In Colossians 4:6a Paul instructs: 'Let your speech always be gracious, seasoned with salt'. Remember Jesus saying that we should be salt and light (Matthew

5:13-16). Saltiness is about flavour – spreading the flavour of the joy of being in a personal relationship with Jesus. Saltiness is about preserving – helping to preserve God's standards. And saltiness is sometimes about being slightly abrasive – in the sense of standing alone to promote what is right! Discuss.

• In Colossians 4:6b Paul adds the explanation: 'So that you may know how you ought to answer everyone.' We need to be filled with the power of the indwelling Holy Spirit to give us the right words for every situation. Discuss.

• In what ways do your *congregations/fellowships* back their ministries with prayer?

A letter to you (A question that is directed specifically to you individually):

• Think about applying the aspirations Paul challenges us with, in your own life. Are there any particular difficulties or fears linked with that? And are there any areas that you particularly need to pray about?

(Afterwards, allow a few minutes for members of the group to share anything that particularly came out of this time of personal meditation for them – if they would like to.)

A letter to God (Pick a prayer that is appropriate for you, personalise it if you would like to and then say it out loud):

Loving, heavenly Father,
Help us to be devoted to prayer: for those in need, for

the ministry of our *fellowships/congregations*, and for our personal witness to others. *(Respecting confidentiality, name specific requests – including people and situations from around the world.)*
In Jesus' name,
Amen.

God of love,
Thank you that you always listen to our prayers and answer them in the best way possible according to your will and purposes.
Help us to have the confidence to pray to you anywhere, about anything – and even to offer prayer as a gift to others. *(Name any particular areas of prayer that you feel nervous or confused about.)*
In Jesus' name,
Amen.

Gracious God,
Thank you for the power of prayer.
Help us to make time to pray; and in that prayer time to offer up everything we do in our *fellowships/congregations* to you. *(Respecting confidentiality, name areas of ministry that are forthcoming, needing the backing of prayer.)*
In Jesus' name,
Amen.

Almighty God,
Thank you that you are our source of wisdom.
Help us to be wise in the way we act towards others. *(Give some examples of the type of occasions that demand such wisdom.)*
In Jesus' name,
Amen.

Heavenly Father,
Thank you for the gift of your Holy Spirit: fill us afresh and empower us for service.
We pray for doors to open so that we might proclaim the gospel clearly.
Help us to make the best of every opportunity you set before us. *(Name any particular qualities that you feel are essential to do that.)*
In Jesus' name,
Amen.

Loving God,
We pray that our conversation might be full of grace and seasoned with salt.
Give us the right words to say in every situation and the right actions to accompany those words. *(Name the type of situations when you might find it difficult to know what to say and do.)*
In Jesus' name,
Amen

Lord Jesus,
You taught us to be salt to the world.
Help us to spread the flavour of the joy of being in a personal relationship with you.
Help us to do our bit to preserve your standards in society.
And help us to be prepared to stand alone to promote what is right.
(Pray for your fellowship/congregation as you jointly and individually strive to be salt in your corner of the world – and for those who you reach out to.)
In your name,
Amen.

Our Lord and Saviour Jesus Christ,
Thank you for those who have been salt to us – maybe
parents, teachers, friends or mentors. *(Encourage members of
the group to silently give thanks to God for specific people who
fit this criteria.)*
In your name,
Amen.

Almighty God,
We pray for the kingdom ...
*(Invite members of the group to name particular aspects of the
kingdom or kingdom building that they feel God has laid upon
their hearts.)*
In Jesus' name,
Amen.

Refreshments and prayer ministry
As you enjoy the time of refreshments together, you might
like to chat about what you feel has particularly stood out
for you from Paul's letter to the Colossians and how you are
going to respond.

Monday
Trapped

Bible readings:
Colossians 4:7-18; Philemon, verses 1-25

Onesimus' story (part 1):
Putting together all the pieces, with a bit of imagination and a degree of licence, Onesimus' story begins like this:

A slight aside! Your initial reaction might be, 'Well that's a very strange name! I don't know anyone called Onesimus! Is it a real name? How do you spell it?'
O-N-E-S-I-M-U-S.
It is a real name; but the question you should be asking is, 'What does the name Onesimus mean?' Now that is an interesting one. The name 'Onesimus' means 'useful'. What a great name! Imagine having the epitaph: 'Onesimus: he lived up to his name.' Sadly, at the start of the story he didn't particularly live up to his name. But I guess, if we are honest, we might fall short of living up to that name!
In many ways Onesimus was much like any other young man, and I know that I am generalising here. But he was in the prime of life, fit, active, ambitious and spirited. As well as that, there was a bit of rebelliousness and fight in him: possibly against the injustices of society, but most definitely with regard to his own life situation. I am reminded of my own childhood and youth, when my brother and I were frequent users of the phrase: 'It's not fair!' Most of the time, it was without justification. However, in Onesimus' case, he

would have had some considerable justification for saying those words. Life probably wasn't that fair for him, for the simple reason that he was a slave – not a very good one – but still a slave. I might add that he was a slave to a respected Christian man called Philemon (a member of the Colossian Church) and he treated Onesimus very well – but it was still a life in captivity.

I said that Onesimus had a bit of fight in him. He had . . . and that's why he so desperately wanted to escape from his situation. He realised that such an act could carry serious consequences, but had reached the point of not caring about that any more. The escape was planned carefully: the day, the time, the method and the route. He had even saved up some food for the journey – and possibly took one or two things that didn't belong to him, as well – but we won't say too much about that at this stage of the story! When everything was ready, he said his 'goodbyes' to those whom he could trust. And then . . . And then he was ready to activate the plan.

Your story (a message for today): Trapped
Have you ever been tempted to delve into your family tree and find out more about your ancestry? Perhaps it is something you have actually done; or maybe you can't be bothered or are apprehensive about what you might discover. Having said that, it must be quite interesting to find out about where we come from and to be able to add a few factual details to some of the names of distant relations.

I feel it's a bit like that with some of the characters in the Bible. There are those whom we know so much about, some that we know little about and those that are mentioned in name only.

In the case of those we know little about, we have to try to piece together small bits of scriptural evidence to get a better idea of their stories. One such character is Onesimus; I've always been fascinated by his inclusion in Scripture. He gets a mention in Colossians 4:9 and his story is told briefly in Paul's letter to Philemon.

As we piece together the metaphorical jigsaw puzzle, we discover that the story begins at the point of Onesimus living in slavery and belonging to Philemon – who is a Christian in the Colossian Church and someone who is well known to Paul. Have you ever thought what it might be like to be a slave? I suspect it would not be a career choice, or even a job to fall back onto when other choices have not worked out. But seriously, to be a slave means living in captivity, the removal of choices, loss of dignity, and maybe suffering different kinds of abuse. Even if your master is a Christian, life as a slave must be extremely difficult.

We laughingly refer to various tasks as 'slave labour'. Sadly, slavery does still go on in different guises today, even in the United Kingdom. It is not necessarily called slavery but it is still happening. I suspect most of us have no idea what it is really like to be a slave.

We're not told much about Onesimus' experience of slavery, but the particular significance of it comes out later on in the story, when he willingly returns to it. Sufficient to say that there is enough in the story to lead us to believe that in the beginning Onesimus is far from happy or contented in his captivity. He is in a place where he really doesn't want to be; doing what he doesn't want to be doing. We can visualise him waking up every morning overcome by feelings of dread. As far as he is concerned, it is another day in captivity, another day performing monotonous, physically draining tasks and another day of pointlessness and hopelessness.

So, what might you dream of if you were living in such captivity? Not such a wild guess: I believe that we, like Onesimus would dream of freedom, which leads us to the deep debate of 'What is true freedom?' If we were to ask Onesimus that question during this first part of his story his reply would probably be something like, 'Freedom for me would be running away from slavery.'

However, you know what people say: 'The thing about unresolved problems is that, if you try to run away from them, they have a habit of following.' We are led to believe later on in Onesimus' story, that his real issues are nothing to do with being in slavery or his lack of freedom.

How often we hear people utter the words: 'If only . . .' Maybe we have said them.

'If only I could move house, everything would be ok then.'

'If only I could change job, there wouldn't be a problem.'

'If only we had more money, life would be great!'

'If only . . .'

Sometimes people have hit the nail on the head: perhaps the house is the problem . . . or the job, or the cash flow! But often the problems are deeper emotional, relationship or spiritual ones. Then, when the 'If only . . .' happens, the person involved is plunged into despair because there has been no benefit whatsoever. That is the tragedy. That could be your scenario, or that of someone close to you.

Onesimus' problems are essentially spiritual: he is trapped and enslaved by things like sin, discontent and hopelessness in his life.

Sin, discontent and hopelessness are real slave masters today – as they always have been! Sin is addictive, controlling and destructive. Small, unchecked sins are just the thin end of the wedge. Discontent and hopelessness are closely related to sin. Freedom of choice – with no restraints – is not freedom!

Though Philemon is a believer, we understand that Onesimus is not a believer at this stage of the story. But that is not to say that Philemon's witness is not having a significant impact on Onesimus' life.

There are times when we sow the seed (witness to those around us in word and deed), but we don't necessarily reap the harvest (have the joy of sharing in that person's experience of coming to Christ). We shouldn't become discouraged or disheartened – and we shouldn't stop witnessing.

I know that it is easy to say (not having been caught up in slavery myself) but Onesimus is entrapped in a worldly viewpoint. He is seeing his situation from the viewpoint of worldly values, rather than God's.

Perhaps you are struggling with your own situation: where you live, the job that you do, the people you mix with, etc. and you are unable to find contentment or hope. We can sometimes be so busy trying to run away from situations that we forget to ask God to reveal the purpose of that situation to us, and how we can glorify him and further his kingdom through it.

There are times when we might have seen a family member, friend, neighbour or colleague – who would not profess to being a believer – going through challenging times. We did all that we could to help in physical and emotional ways but felt that they needed more. Maybe at the time someone commented, or it might even have gone through our minds: What they need is a personal relationship with Jesus.

It might almost seem a bit flippant – but it is true. Nothing is as life-changing, in a positive way, than a personal relationship with Jesus. It enables us to endure the hardships and difficulties of life; it brings a point to the pointless and brings hope to the hopeless.

What Onesimus really needs at this stage in his life is a personal relationship with Jesus!

What we all really need is a personal relationship with Jesus – if we haven't already got one!

Key thoughts about being trapped:

- Sin, discontent and hopelessness are real slave masters today.

- Freedom of choice – with no restraints – is not freedom!

- What we all really need is a personal relationship with Jesus!

Resting in prayer:

Be still and quiet in God's presence in an attitude of thankfulness for the freedom that Jesus offers.

Tuesday
Running away

Bible reading:
The Book of Jonah

Onesimus' story (part 2):
Last time we left Onesimus just about to activate his escape plan. Now we join him halfway into his journey:

It had seemed like a good idea to run away from being Philemon's slave, but Onesimus was reaching the stage of beginning to have a few regrets. The days were hot; the roads were dry and dusty; the terrain was hazardous; he was tired, hungry and thirsty; though he knew the direction he was heading in (Rome), he didn't know where he would be able to stay once he arrived; and he was fearful. He was afraid of every footstep and hoof beat that he heard approaching from behind – just in case! It could be someone who had been sent out to capture him and return him to Philemon – or worse! Onesimus came to the sudden realisation that escaping captivity had neither met his expectations nor given him a feeling of true freedom. He felt a sinking feeling in the depths of his stomach: a feeling of panic and despair.

The blisters on Onesimus' feet told a tale. In those days there were no aeroplanes, trains, buses, cars, motorcycles or even the humble pedal cycle . . . besides he had no money anyway. And Onesimus didn't possess or have access to a donkey or camel. Every inch of the journey was on foot and by this stage it had reached the point of every footstep being accompanied with intense pain – thanks to multiple blisters. Onesimus began to wonder if the venture could ever be worth the pain, anxiety or fear.

Your story (a message for today)**:** Running away
In the world of fiction, there is an element of glamour and excitement attached to running away. In the real world that is not the case. Running away from problems is not the answer; it doesn't solve anything.

Despite running away from slavery in Philemon's household, Onesimus is still not a free man – he is a captive on the run! There is a suggestion that Onesimus has taken either money or possessions from Philemon (maybe another reason for him running away) – so he is also a thief on the run. It is possible that a third reason for Onesimus running away is that God is beginning to challenge him through the witness of Philemon. But you can't run away from God! Onesimus is not free!

In the twenty-first century, people search for true freedom: freedom from guilt, freedom from regrets, freedom from feelings of rejection, freedom from feelings of inadequacy and freedom from hopelessness. But in the relentless search for freedom and inner peace, people so often look in the wrong places: self-centred ambition, greed and materialism, lust and other forms of self-indulgence, addictions, etc. – but nothing in a Christian context. Nothing truly sets free or satisfies except the Triune God: God the Father, Jesus the Son and the Holy Spirit. A personal relationship with Jesus is the only way to enter into true freedom. We will discover more about that later on in our journey through the letter to Philemon.

There are consequences to our actions and Onesimus has a penalty to pay for stealing. We will discover later in our journey through the letter to Philemon that the penalty is paid by Paul. There is a penalty to pay for our sin: a penalty that has been paid by Jesus.

Onesimus cannot run away from God. We will discover later on in our journey through the letter to Philemon that despite running to Rome – possibly trying to run away from the witness of Philemon – Onesimus is greeted by the witness of Paul.

In comparison, I am sure that we are all familiar with the story of Jonah. God calls Jonah to go to Nineveh to warn the people there that if they don't repent of their sin and turn back to God there will be serious consequences. Jonah doesn't want to go to Nineveh, or to pass on such a message, so he decides to try to run away from God, by going to Tarshish. He proceeds to Joppa, where he boards a ship going to that port. There is a storm; Jonah realises that it is because he is trying to run away from God, and allows the sailors to throw him overboard. Jonah is swallowed by a big fish. He spends a long time in prayer. Three days and nights later, the fish deposits Jonah on dry land; God once again instructs him to go to Nineveh and this time Jonah obeys.

Jonah discovers that it is impossible to run away from God. He learns the same lesson as Onesimus. The same lesson applies to us today: you and I really cannot run away from God. God is all-seeing, all-knowing and all-present. We can't hide our sins from God: he is all-seeing. We can't pull the wool over God's eyes: he knows everything about us. We can't run away from the calling of God: he will be right behind us.

Maybe there is some kind of sin in your life that you have never really dealt with. It needs dealing with right now!

Maybe you think you can hold onto interests or activities in your life that are not glorifying to God – or beneficial to your Christian life – thinking that God won't notice. He will!

Maybe God is calling you to a particular work for him and you're drawing back from it. You can't run away from God!

Maybe you have been running away from God all your life and have never entered into a personal relationship with Jesus. Stop running!

To close . . . there is a very positive side to not being able to run away from God. God is in control. God never gives up on any of us. Even if we stupidly try to go our own way and turn our backs on God – momentarily, or for a longer spell of time – God never leaves us for a moment. We can run as much as we like but as soon as we reach out to God, he will be there.

Key thoughts about running away:

- There is a penalty to pay for our sin: a penalty that has been paid for by Jesus.

- We can't pull the wool over God's eyes: he knows everything about us.

- We can't run away from God!

- God never gives up on any of us.

Resting in prayer:
Be still and quiet in God's presence in an attitude of thankfulness that God never gives up on us.

Wednesday
Found

Bible reading:
1 Corinthians 12:12-31

Onesimus' story (part 3):
Yesterday we left Onesimus on his journey to Rome in which not everything was straightforward. Today we join Onesimus as he arrives at his destination:

We speak about chance meetings, don't we? But is there really such a thing in God's plan? Rome was a big place, lots of buildings and people. And yet out of all those crowds of men, women and children, who should Onesimus bump into but the New Testament evangelist and writer, Paul. He was someone who maybe could understand something of how Onesimus had been feeling whilst in the captivity of being a slave because Paul himself was being held in the captivity of house arrest. That being the case, Onesimus must have bumped into someone who invited him to come along and meet Paul – and listen to his wonderful words of personal testimony and stories about Jesus.

Such was Paul's witness in word and deed that it wasn't long before he had the joy of leading Onesimus into meeting with Jesus, saying sorry for the things he had done wrong and entering into a personal relationship of faith with him. What a joy!

Your story (a message for today): Found

I am sure that we have all had the experience of bumping into someone unexpectedly: maybe a friend or colleague, or someone we have never met before. Conversation develops. You are able to say something that the other person really needs to hear at that point of time, or the other person is able to say something to you that you really need to hear. Afterwards you feel that it was 'meant to be'!

I recall a lady, who I barely knew, giving me a big hug in the middle of a car park – because she sensed that I needed a hug after the loss of a loved pet minutes beforehand.

Nothing is by chance with God!

Onesimus' meeting with Paul is not a 'chance meeting'! It is part of God's plan for Onesimus to meet with Paul in Rome and no coincidence that somehow, in the whole of Rome, their paths cross. And it is during Onesimus' time with Paul that he comes to faith.

Jeremiah 29:11 tells us that God has a plan for each of our lives: 'For surely I know the plans I have for you, says the Lord, plans for your welfare and not for harm, to give you a future with hope.' With God, nothing is by coincidence. When we have a personal relationship with Jesus, and are willing to do things God's way, he will work out that plan in and through us. God's plan is perfect. There is a reason for everything; even if we don't immediately understand what it is. And there is something good in every situation, if we look for it. God has the advantage of seeing the larger picture. That's one of the reasons we can trust him with our lives. And God's timing is perfect.

Let's think about the nature of true repentance. We are led to believe that Onesimus has been lazy and 'useless' to Philemon. We are led to believe that Onesimus has stolen from Philemon. And we are also led to believe that Onesimus' conduct has not been glorifying to God or furthering of his kingdom.

Onesimus comes to the point of repentance. True repentance is not just to say 'sorry' but to have the intention of not doing the same things wrong again. It's about wanting to improve and to live a better life: one that is glorifying to God and furthering of his kingdom – a 'useful' life.

Through meeting with Paul – his witness and example – Onesimus enters into a personal relationship with Jesus. Following Jesus is all about striving to understand and live by Jesus' teaching and example, and striving to take on the characteristics of Jesus, to become more Christlike. It is also about following his leading; being clothed in his righteousness; made fit for God's heavenly kingdom and being filled with the empowering Holy Spirit.

Onesimus becomes different through his personal relationship with Jesus. He has a transformed approach and attitude to life. He is useful to Paul, so much so, that Paul wants him to remain with him. Onesimus and Paul form a close friendship held together through the faith that they have in common. Jesus transforms lives for the better.

Through faith in Jesus, we are joined together as part of the family of God: sharing fellowship with God and each other, praying together, studying the Scriptures together, worshipping God together, growing spiritually together and serving together.

Key thoughts about being found:

- Nothing is by chance with God!

- God has a plan for each of our lives.

- Jesus transforms lives for the better.

- Through faith in Jesus, we are joined together as part of the family of God

Resting in prayer:
Be still and quiet in God's presence in an attitude of thankfulness that God has a plan for each of our lives, which involves being part of his family.

Thursday
Serving

Bible reading:
Luke 8:26-39

Onesimus' story (part 4):
Yesterday, we left the story with Onesimus having just given his life to Jesus. What next?

Paul had become good friends with Onesimus and in one sense would have been only too happy to have him stay with him indefinitely. He was good company, a willing helper and a committed Christian. But both Paul and Onesimus realised that it wouldn't be the right thing to do.

Onesimus felt that God had placed him into the household of Philemon in order to serve Jesus in that place. How? Simply by endeavouring to be the best slave ever: honest, hardworking, cooperative, compassionate and reliable . . . and by sharing his personal experience of meeting with Jesus with those around him.

Paul was willing to let his new friend go, in the knowledge of him returning to his master, with the intention of fulfilling his God-given calling. But, Paul was concerned that Onesimus' return should be a positive event and would lead to rejoicing in Philemon's household. So, being as Paul knew Philemon well – What a coincidence! – I think not! – he wrote a letter for Onesimus to take back with him.

Dear Philemon,

Long time no see! It's not through the want of coming to see you.

I send my dear friend Onesimus back to you. I would love to have kept him here in Rome with me but it is right that he should return to you. I need to tell you that he's not the same person who left you in such anger, laziness and discontentment. He has been saved by entering into a personal relationship with Jesus – so he returns to you as a brother in Christ.

If he has stolen anything from you in the past, I will pay it back to you. I know you will treat him well.

Yours in Christ,
Paul.

Your story (a message for today): Serving
Have you ever attended some kind of special occasion? It may have been a prize-giving at school, an AGM for an organisation you are linked with, some kind of celebration or open day for a place of work, a wedding etc. The time comes for the speeches and maybe a presentation of awards and you are sitting thinking, 'I wonder if I will get a mention,' or, 'I wonder if I will get an award.' And you don't! Most of us have probably been there at some time or another.

It's quite something that Onesimus gets a mention in the Bible to be remembered throughout future generations. But what is so special about him, that amongst all the thousands of early converts, he gets a mention? Onesimus would appear to be a very ordinary person and I don't mean that in a disrespectful way. We would assume that he is uneducated and he has no wealth of his own. We know that he has no particular position or authority. And though the name 'Onesimus' means useful, without judging him, we know that he starts out as being a useless slave and eventually runs away. We assume from the story that Onesimus is not even honest in the time leading up to him running away. Even after his conversion, Onesimus doesn't appear to become a great New Testament evangelist, missionary, church leader or apostle. Maybe it is for the encouragement and affirmation of those of us who at times feel insignificant in God's plan and unworthy of mention or reward. Maybe it is for those of us who live quite ordinary lives, whose callings involve doing ordinary things, and who are called to be Jesus' hands and feet in very ordinary places and situations.

At this final stage of the story, Onesimus could be forgiven for imagining that God is calling him to stay with Paul and become a missionary – that God has led him to Rome for this very purpose. I am sure that Onesimus' decision to return to Philemon's household is not one he makes lightly. And I'm certain that both Paul and Onesimus only make the decision after praying for discernment from God.

The story of Onesimus highlights a number of things after his conversion that we should apply to our own Christian lives.

The importance of humility: The Christian life is not about power, authority, celebrity status or financial gain. And it is not about seeking favour, recognition or reward. It is about willingly doing those things that often go unnoticed by others; it is about giving the glory to God. Onesimus is prepared to go back to life as a slave. Life doesn't get much humbler than that, I am sure!

The nature of service: Service is about putting others first, before self. I suspect that it is something Onesimus struggles with, before meeting with Jesus. But leading up to his return to Philemon the situation has turned around. Onesimus is happy to serve Paul in any way he can; so much so, that Paul doesn't want to part with him. At long last Onesimus is living up to his name: Useful!

That we should strive to glorify God in everything: We should all endeavour to glorify God in our lives. Almost any job can be done in such a way that it glorifies God: by working hard and conscientiously, by conducting our work with honesty and integrity, and by having the right motivation, values and goals. I am sure that with Jesus as his Lord and Saviour Onesimus goes back to Philemon eager to perform his old tasks in such a way that he will glorify God.

The power of witness: Remember the story about Legion! Jesus doesn't let him travel with him; instead, he sends Legion back home to witness to those who know what he was like before becoming a believer and experiencing Jesus' power in his life. Sometimes our greatest witness is to those around us: friends, family, work colleagues, neighbours and those we socialise with. Sometimes the mission field to which we are called is in our own backyards – right where God has placed us already! I suspect that Onesimus' greatest witness is to be amongst those who remember him as an idle, useless slave.

Calling: Our callings aren't always the callings we would choose: the nature of the things God calls us to do, the location, or the people with whom we are called to work. Onesimus is willing to be where God wants him to be, doing the things God wants him to be doing. We should respond to our callings in the same way.

Contentment: The key to finding contentment is linked with being in God's will. I believe that when Onesimus returns to

Philemon he manages to find contentment in the situation where God has placed him.

Commitment: An essential part of the Christian faith is commitment: to the Triune God, and to prayer, Bible study, worship, witness and service. We assume that Onesimus returns to Philemon and manages to be really committed to serving God in the situation where God has placed him.

Having the price paid by another: Jesus has paid the penalty for our sin. Paul promises to pay anything that is owing to Philemon.

Forgiveness and restoration: We are forgiven and restored in our relationship with the Triune God, through our personal relationship with Jesus, based on repentance and faith. I believe that forgiveness and restoration take place between Onesimus and Philemon.

The family of God: Through our relationship with Jesus, we become part of God's family. Paul points out to Philemon that though Onesimus is his slave, he is also a brother in Christ.

We have seen God's plan for Onesimus unfold before us. And God is also working out his plan for each one of us – if we are prepared to allow him to – in faith.

Key thoughts about serving:

- We might be called to be Jesus' hands and feet in very ordinary places and situations.

- Almost any job can be done in such a way that it glorifies God: by working hard and conscientiously, by conducting our work with honesty and integrity, and by having the right motivation, values and goals.

- We are forgiven and restored in our relationship with the Triune God, through our personal relationship with Jesus, based on repentance and faith.

- God is working out his plan for each one of us – if we are prepared to allow him to – in faith.

Resting in prayer:
Be still and quiet in God's presence in an attitude of thankfulness for the privilege of serving.

Friday
Prayer response

Bible readings:
Luke 23:26-43; Philemon, verses 1-25

Key thoughts about being trapped:

- Sin, discontent and hopelessness are real slave masters today.

- Freedom of choice – with no restraints – is not freedom!

- What we all really need is a personal relationship with Jesus!

Lord and Saviour Jesus Christ,
Thank you that you love us all unconditionally.
Thank you that you suffered and died on the cross, paying
the penalty for sin.
Thank you that you rose again and want to have a personal
relationship with each one of us.
Thank you that when we follow you, you forgive us, you
help us to discover true contentment and you fill us with
eternal hope.
Thank you that you are the source of true freedom.
Please forgive me when I fall short of the Father's standards
and expectations.
Give me the wisdom to make good choices.
Fill me afresh with the power of your indwelling Holy Spirit
and help me to allow him complete freedom to work in my life.
Grant me contentment.

Fill me with the hope of eternal life in your heavenly kingdom.
Help me to walk closer to you, day by day.
And help me to live a life that is glorifying to God and will
point others towards you.
I *commit/recommit* my life to you.
In his name,
Amen.

Key thoughts about running away:

- There is a penalty to pay for our sin: a penalty that has
  been paid for by Jesus.

- We can't pull the wool over God's eyes: he knows
  everything about us.

- We can't run away from God!

- God never gives up on any of us.

Loving, heavenly Father,
Thank you that you love and care about us all.
Thank you that we can't run away from you, even though
we might try to sometimes; and we can't pull the wool over
your eyes, because you know everything there is to know
about each one of us.
Thank you that you have provided the way to salvation, and
you never give up on any of us.
Please help me not to waste time in trying to run away from
you. Instead, help me to be obedient to your will for me.
I *submit/resubmit* myself to your will.
In Jesus' name,
Amen.

Key thoughts about being found:

- Nothing is by chance with God!
- God has a plan for each of our lives.
- Jesus transforms lives for the better.
- Through faith in Jesus, we are joined together as part of the family of God.

Creator God,
Thank you that you created us in your image and that you have a plan for each of our lives – an eternal plan.
Thank you that you are in control of everything.
Thank you that through our relationship with Jesus we are forgiven, cleansed, restored in our relationship with you, progressively transformed more into the likeness of Jesus and filled with amazing peace and eternal hope.
It is so good to be part of your family as a result.
Please enable me to fulfil your plan for me.
Fill me/fill me afresh with your Holy Spirit.
Help me to allow the Holy Spirit to work fully in my life.
In Jesus' name,
Amen.

Key thoughts about serving:

- We might be called to be Jesus' hands and feet in very ordinary places and situations.
- Almost any job can be done in such a way that it glorifies God: by working hard and conscientiously, by conducting our work with honesty and integrity, and by having the right motivation, values and goals.

- We are forgiven and restored in our relationship with the Triune God, through our personal relationship with Jesus, based on repentance and faith.

- God is working out his plan for each one of us – if we are prepared to allow him to – in faith.

Lord Jesus,
Thank you for the privilege of being able to serve you in continuing your work here on earth.
Please fill me with your love and compassion to share with others.
Help me in all that I say and do to point others towards you.
I pray for those who are still seeking inner peace, contentment, freedom and eternal hope. I pray that they might hear about your love for us, this Easter – and respond in a positive way.
I offer up/reoffer up my life to you in service.
In your name,
Amen.

Resting in prayer:
Be still and quiet in God's presence in an attitude of thankfulness that Jesus loves us so much that he gave his life on the cross for us – but he rose again and is alive today, and wants to be in a relationship with us all.